POP PIANO HITS

SIMPLE ARRANGEMENTS FOR STUDENTS OF ALL AGES

Love Yourself, Stitches & More Hot Singles

ISBN 978-1-4950-6231-5

HAL•LEONARD®
CORPORATION
7777 W. BLUEMOUND RD. P.O. BOX 13819 MILWAUKEE, WI 53213

Visit Hal Leonard Online at
www.halleonard.com

LOVE YOURSELF

Words and Music by JUSTIN BIEBER,
BENJAMIN LEVIN and ED SHEERAN

Moderate Ballad

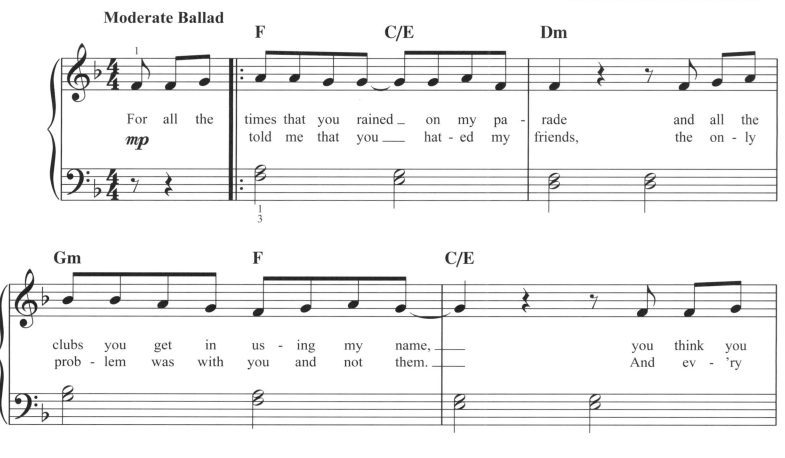

For all the times that you rained on my pa-rade, and all the
told me that you hat-ed my friends, the on-ly

clubs you get in us-ing my name, you think you
prob-lem was with you and not them. And ev-'ry

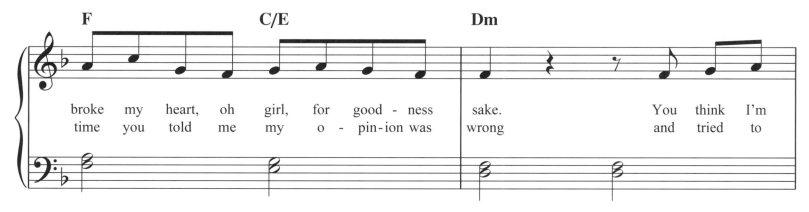

broke my heart, oh girl, for good-ness sake. You think I'm
time you told me my o-pin-ion was wrong and tried to

cry-ing on my own, well I ain't. And I did-n't want to
make me for-get where I was from.

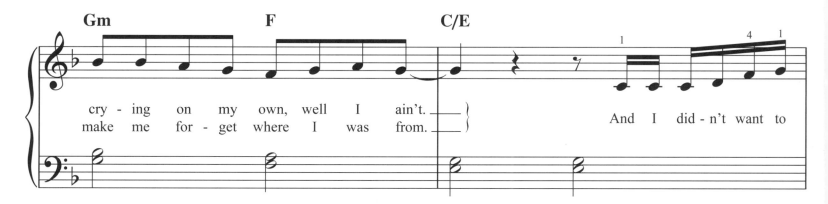

3

write a song ___ 'cause I did-n't want an-y-one think-ing I still care. I

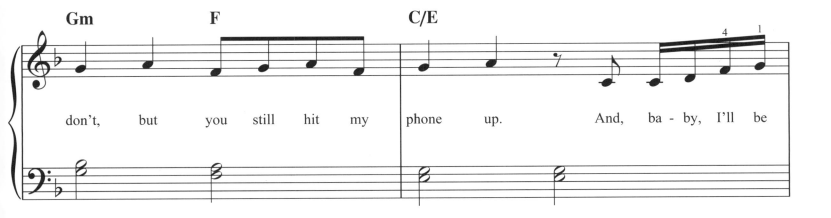

don't, but you still hit my phone up. And, ba-by, I'll be

mov-ing on ___ and I think it should be some-thing I don't want to

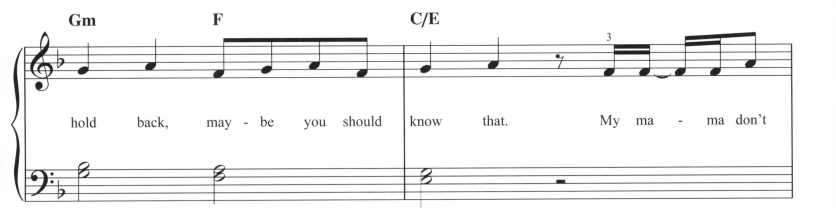

hold back, may-be you should know that. My ma-ma don't

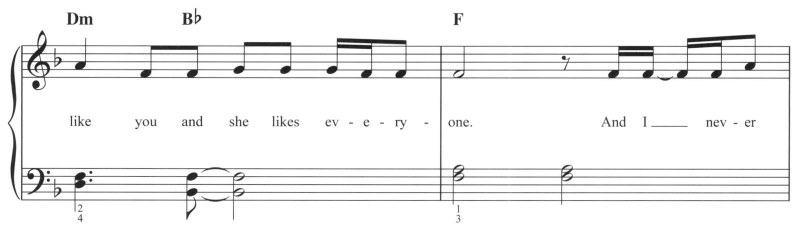

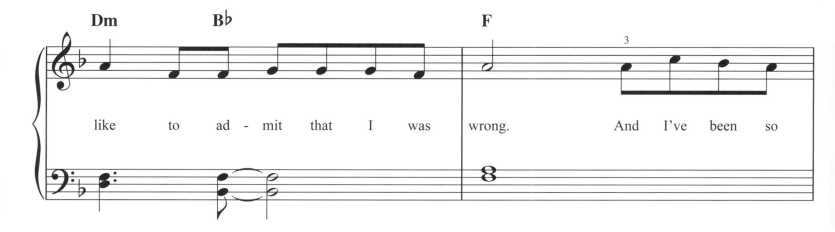

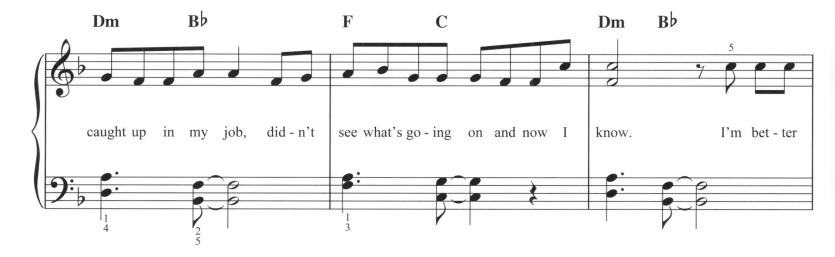

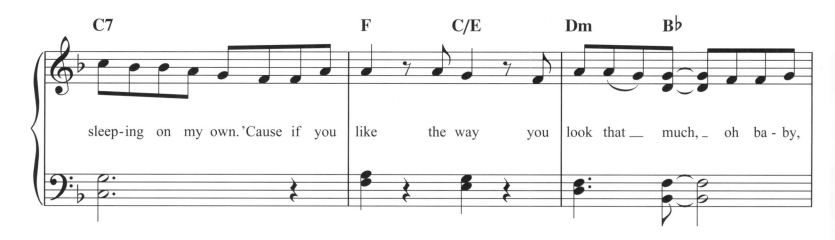

you should go and love your - self. ____ And if you think that I'm still

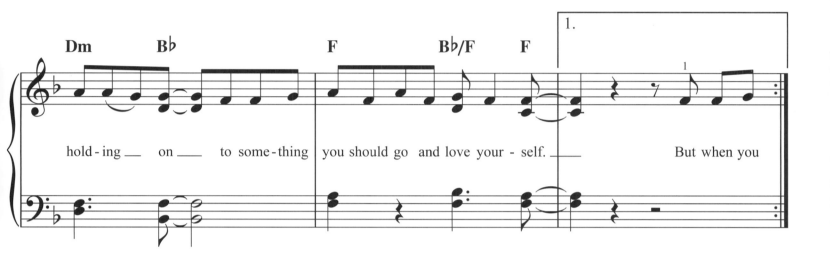

hold - ing __ on __ to some - thing you should go and love your - self. ____ But when you

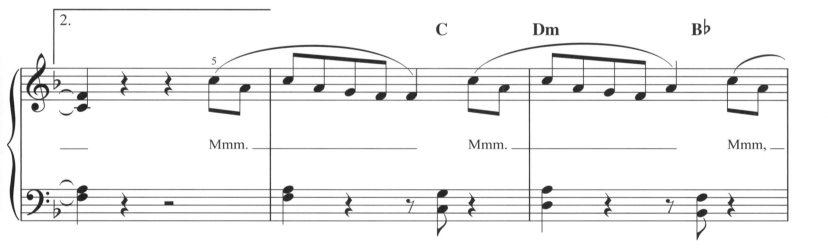

__ Mmm. _____ Mmm. _____ Mmm, __

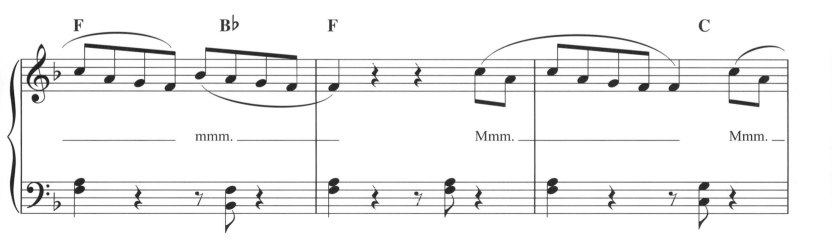

_____ mmm. _____ Mmm. _____ Mmm. __

Mmm, _____ mmm. _____ For all the

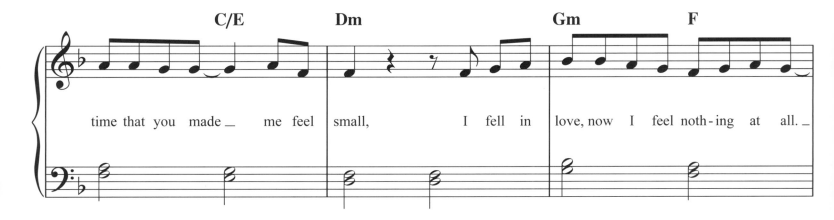

time that you made _ me feel small, I fell in love, now I feel noth-ing at all. _

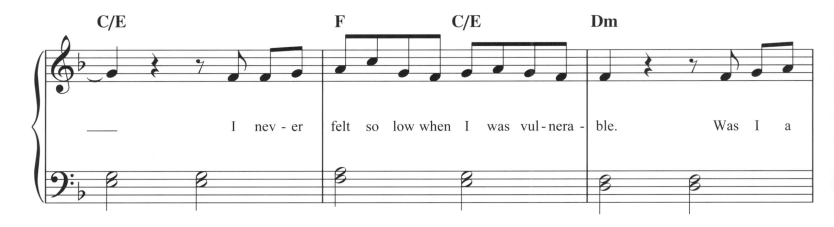

_ I nev - er felt so low when I was vul-nera - ble. Was I a

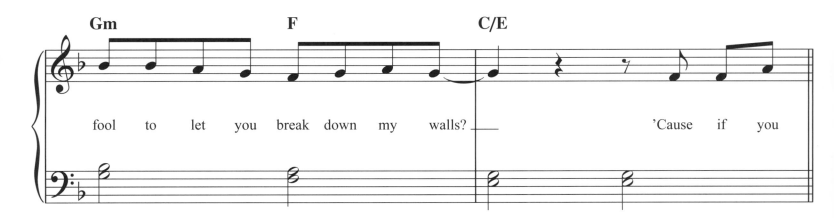

fool to let you break down my walls? _ 'Cause if you

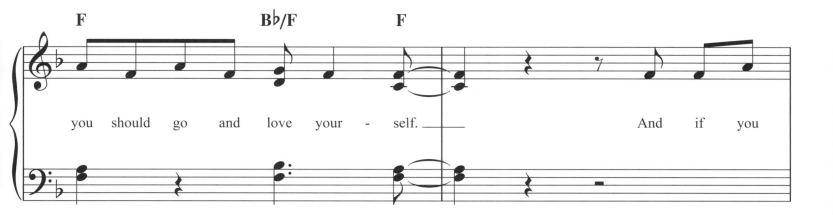

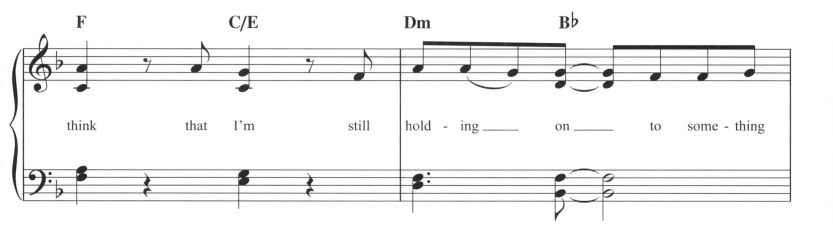

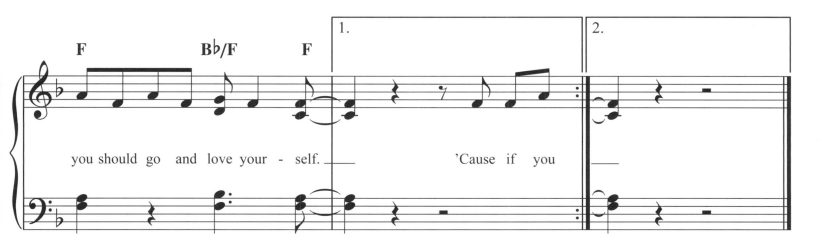

ONE CALL AWAY

Words and Music by CHARLIE PUTH,
BREYAN ISAAC, MATT PRIME,
JUSTIN FRANKS, BLAKE ANTHONY CARTER
and MAUREEN McDONALD

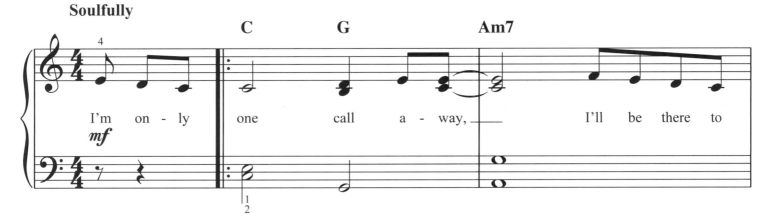

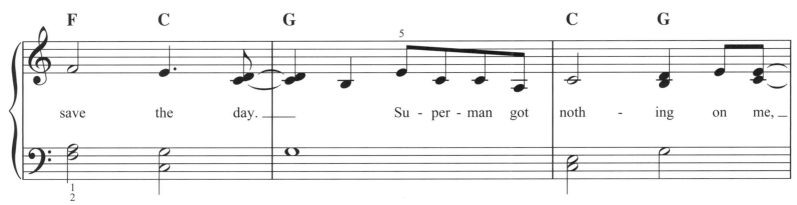

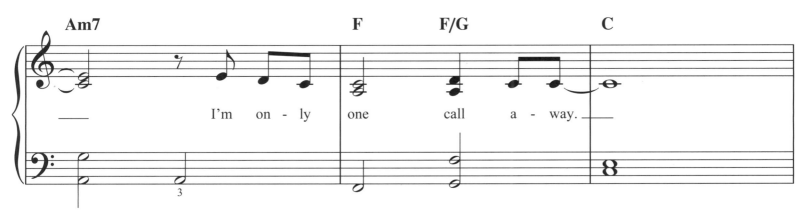

mat-ter where _ you go, you know you're not _ a-lone. I'm on-ly _ one call a-way, _

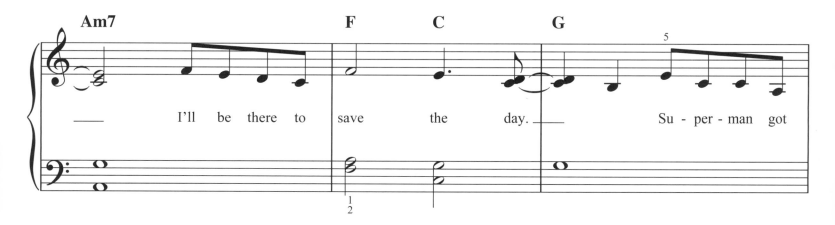

_ I'll be there to save the day. _ Su-per-man got

noth - ing on me, _ I'm on-ly one call a - way. _

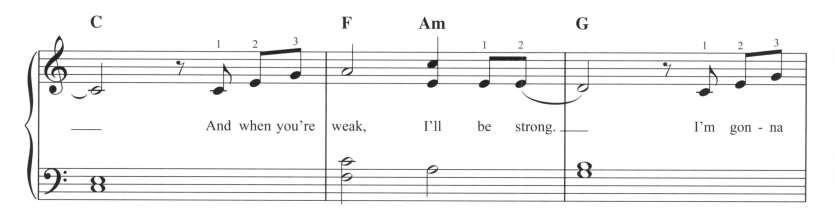

And when you're weak, I'll be strong. _ I'm gon-na

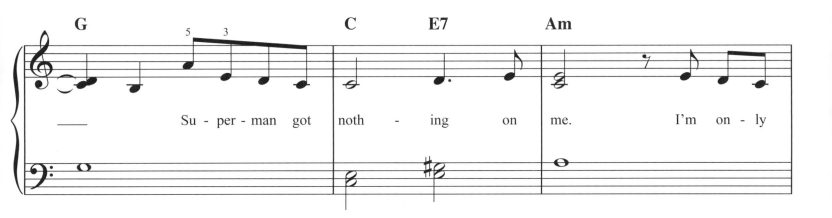

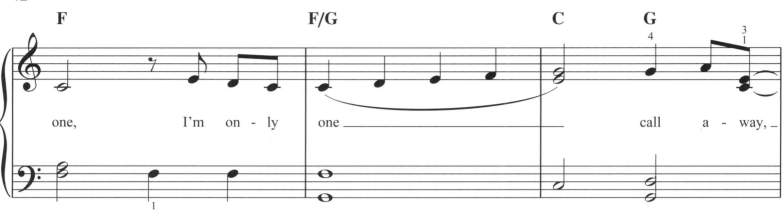

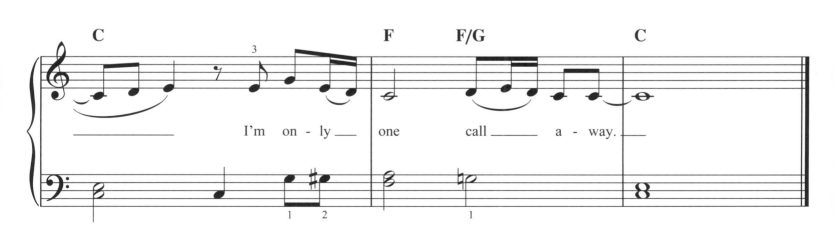

LIKE I'M GONNA LOSE YOU

Words and Music by CAITLYN ELIZABETH SMITH,
JUSTIN WEAVER and MEGHAN TRAINOR

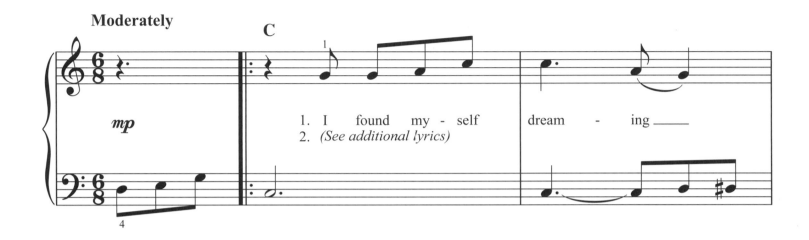

Moderately

C

mp

1. I found my-self dream - ing _____
2. *(See additional lyrics)*

Em

Am

in sil - ver and gold, _____ like a scene from a

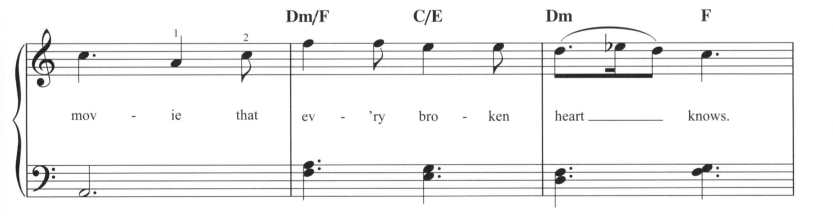

Dm/F   C/E   Dm   F

mov - ie that ev - 'ry bro - ken heart _____ knows.

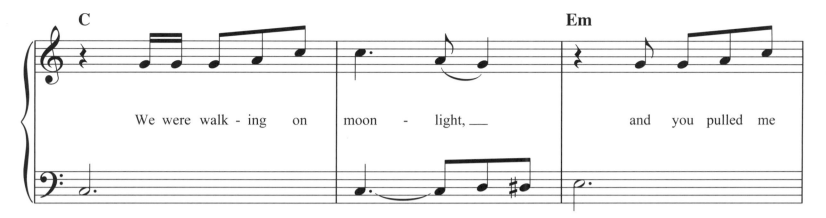

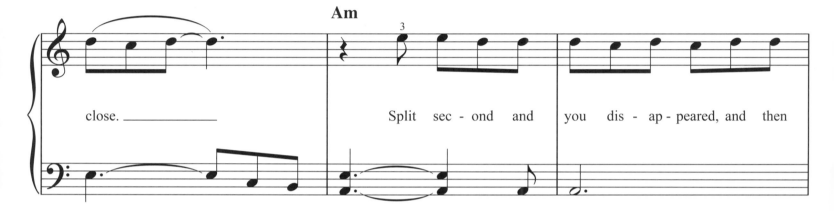

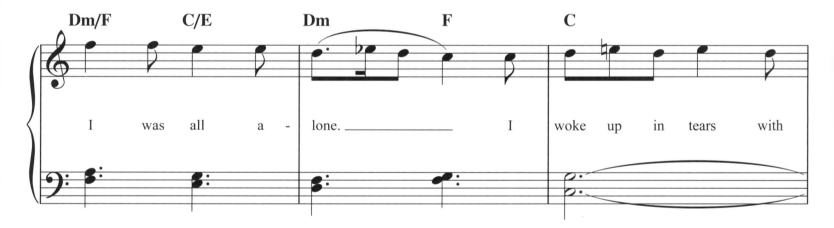

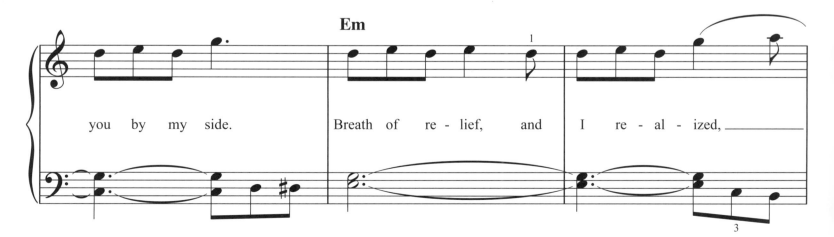

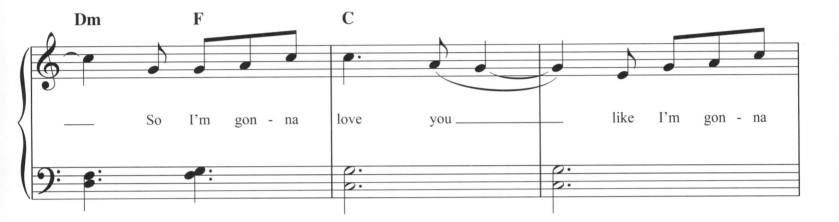

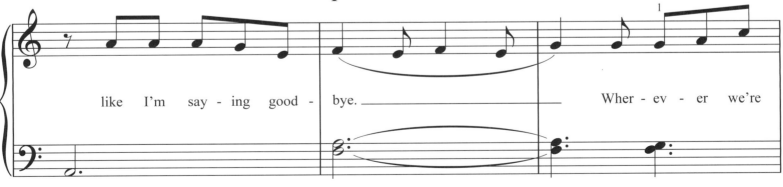

16

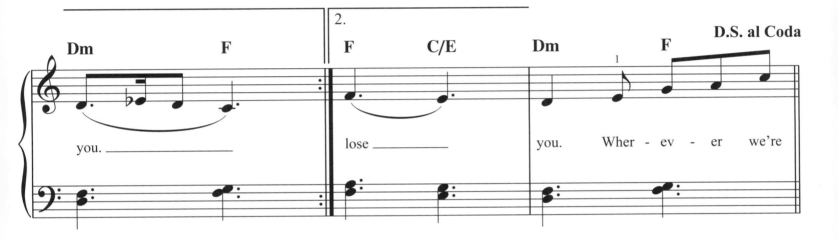

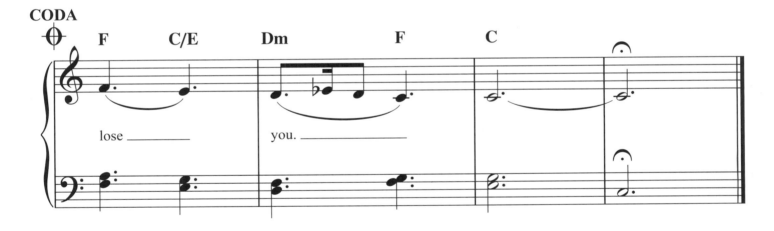

Additional Lyrics

2. In the blink of an eye, just a whisper of smoke,
You could lose ev'rything; the truth is you never know.
So, I'll kiss you longer, baby, any chance that I get.
I'll make the most of the minutes and love with no regret.
Let's take our time to say what we want,
Use what we've got before it's all gone;
'Cause, no, we're not promised tomorrow.

STITCHES

Words and Music by TEDDY GEIGER,
DANNY PARKER and DANIEL KYRIAKIDES

Moderate Latin groove

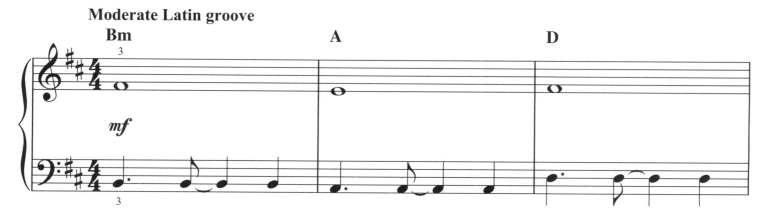

19

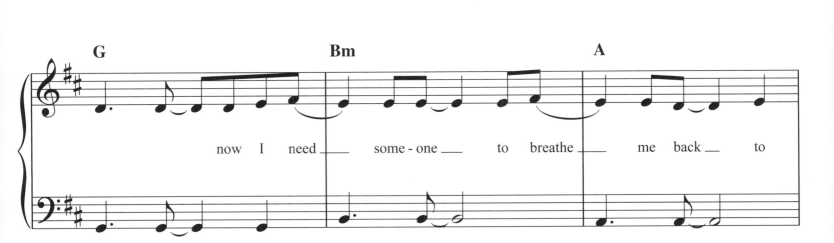

if I quit call-ing you my lov-er and move on.

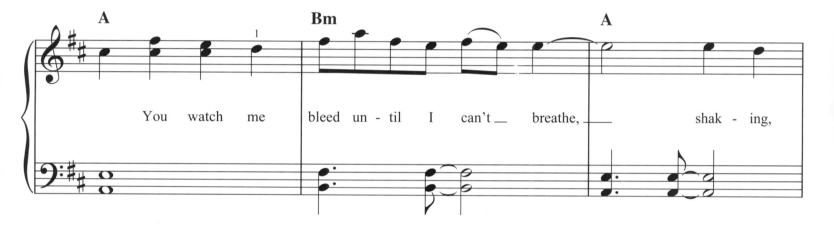

You watch me bleed un-til I can't breathe, shak-ing,

fall-ing on-to my knees. And now that I'm with-out your

kiss-es, I'll be need-ing stitch-es.

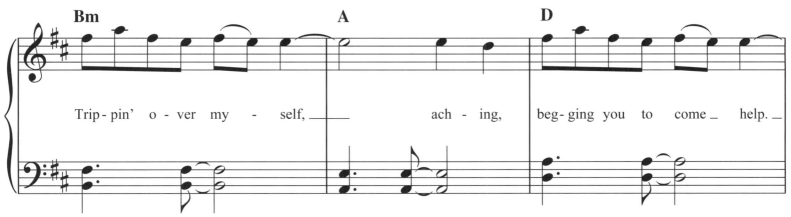

Bm · A · D

Trip-pin' o - ver my - self, _____ ach - ing, beg- ging you to come _ help. _

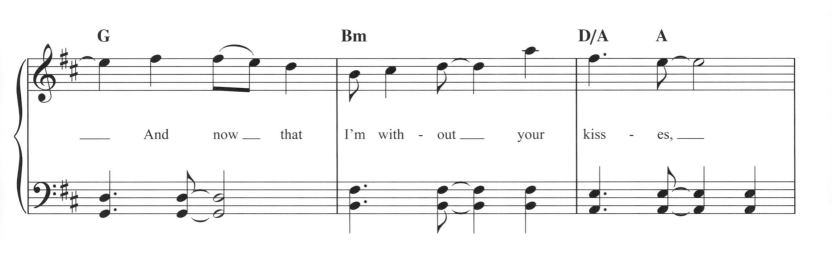

G · Bm · D/A · A

_ And now _ that I'm with - out _ your kiss - es, _

To Coda ⊕

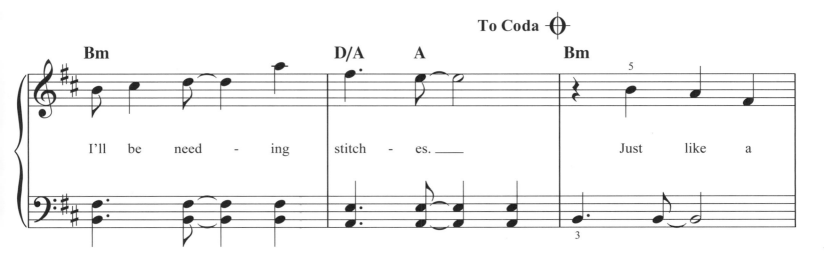

Bm · D/A · A · Bm

I'll be need - ing stitch - es. _ Just like a

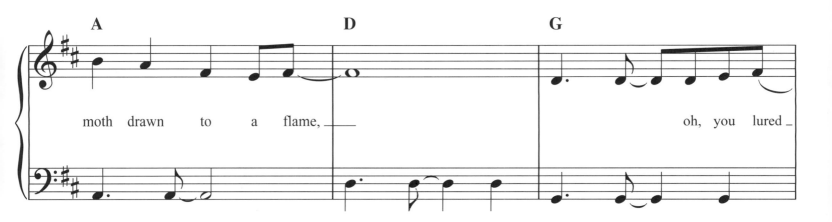

A · D · G

moth drawn to a flame, _ oh, you lured _

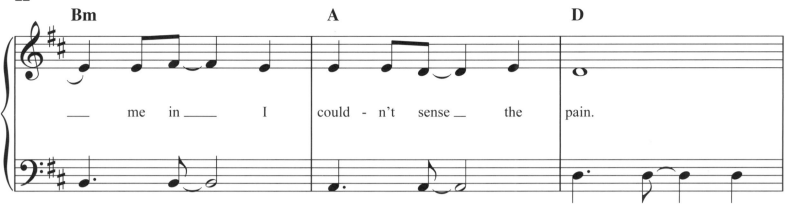

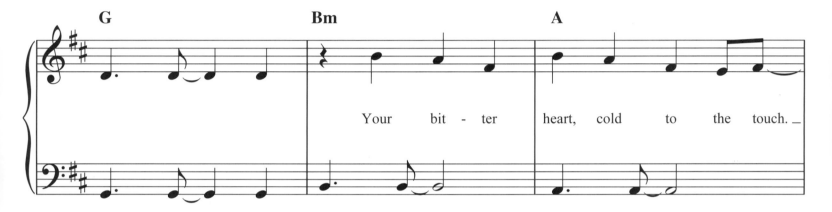

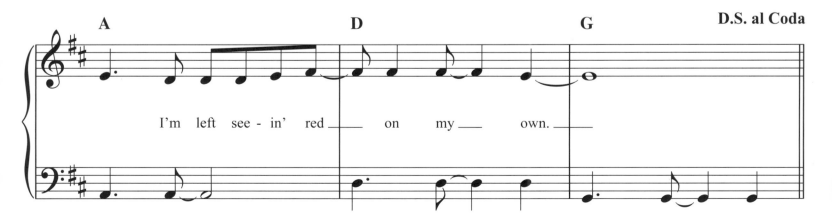

CODA

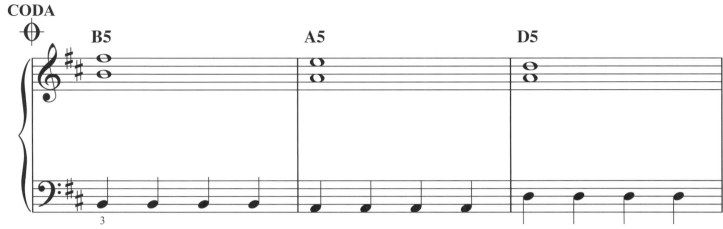

Nee - dle and the thread, got - ta get you out of my head.

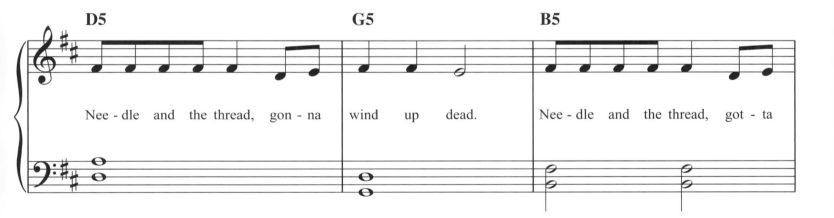

Nee - dle and the thread, gon - na wind up dead. Nee - dle and the thread, got - ta

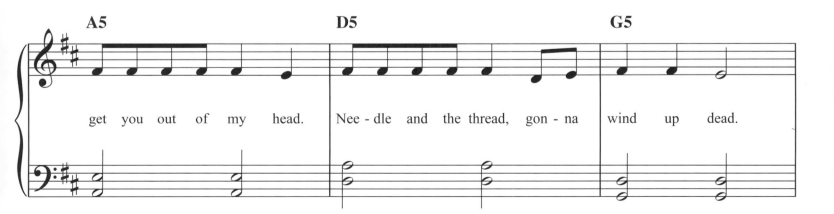

get you out of my head. Nee - dle and the thread, gon - na wind up dead.

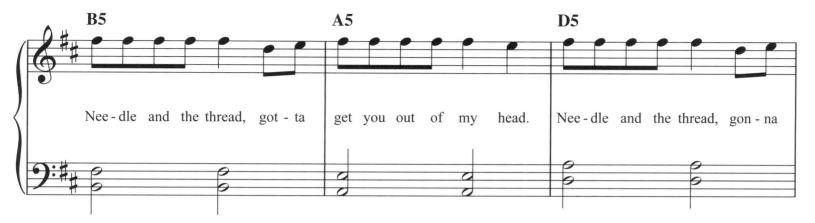

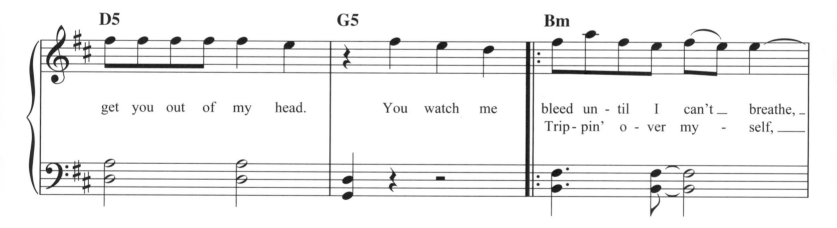

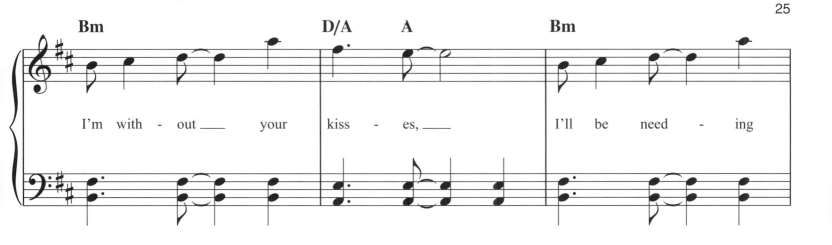

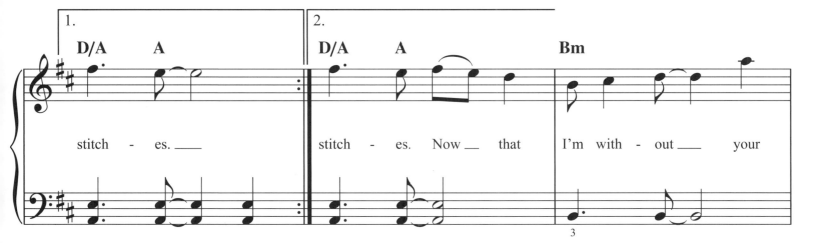

STRESSED OUT

Words and Music by
TYLER JOSEPH

Rap 1: *(See additional lyrics)*

My name's Blur-ry-face, and I care what you think. My name's

27

Rap 2: *(See additional lyrics)*

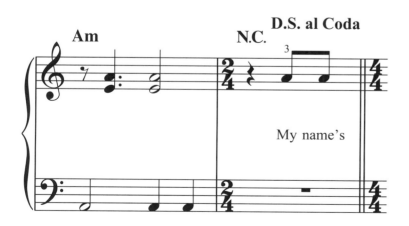

D.S. al Coda

My name's

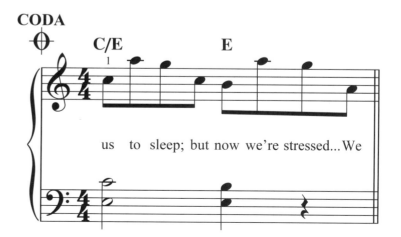

CODA

us to sleep; but now we're stressed...We

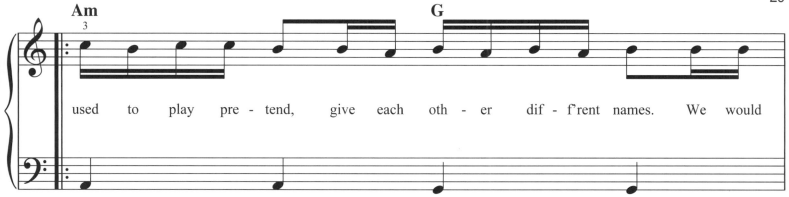

used to play pre - tend, give each oth - er dif - f'rent names. We would

build a rock - et ship and then we'd fly it far a - way. Used to

dream of out - er space, but now they're laugh - in' at our face, say - in',

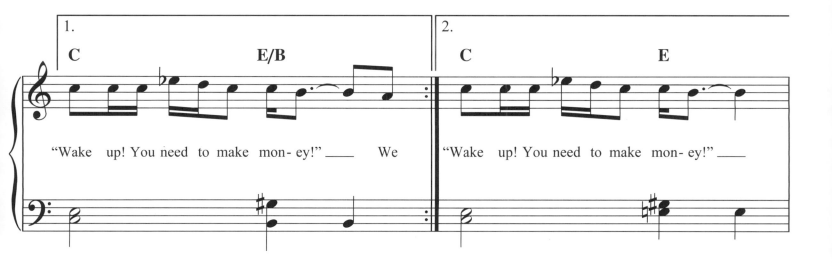

1.
"Wake up! You need to make mon- ey!" ____ We

2.
"Wake up! You need to make mon- ey!" ____

Wish we could turn back time to the good old days, when the mom-ma sang

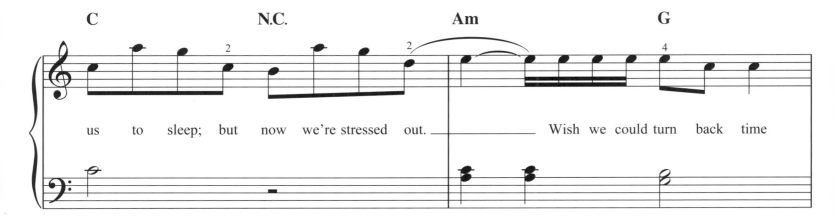

us to sleep; but now we're stressed out. _____ Wish we could turn back time

to the good old days, when the mom-ma sang us to sleep; but now we're stressed out. _

Rap 3: *(See additional lyrics)*

(Wake up! You need to make mon - ey!)

Additional Lyrics

Rap 1: I wish I found better sounds no one's ever heard.
I wish I had a better voice that sang some better words.
I wish I found some chords in an order that is new.
I wish I didn't have to rhyme every time I sang.

I was told when I get older all my fears would shrink,
But now I'm insecure and I care what people think.

Rap 2: Sometimes a certain smell will take me back to when I was young.
How come I'm never able to identify where it's coming from?
I'd make a candle out of it if I ever found it,
Try to sell it, never sell out of it. I'd probably only sell one.

It'd be to my brother, 'cause we have the same nose,
Same clothes, homegrown, a stone's throw from a creek we used to roam.
But it would remind us of when nothing really mattered.
Out of student loans and treehouse homes, we all would take the latter.

Rap 3: We used to play pretend, used to play pretend, bunny.
We used to play pretend; wake up, you need the money.
We used to play pretend, used to play pretend, bunny.
We used to play pretend; wake up, you need the money.

We used to play pretend, give each other different names;
We would build a rocket ship and then we'd fly it far away.
Used to dream of outer space, but now they're laughing at our face,
Saying, "Wake up, you need to make money?" Yo.

POP PIANO HITS

Pop Piano Hits is a series designed for students of all ages. Each book contains five simple and easy-to-read arrangements of today's most popular downloads. Lyrics, fingering and chord symbols are included to help you make the most of each arrangement. Enjoy your favorite songs and artists today!

BLANK SPACE, I REALLY LIKE YOU & MORE HOT SINGLES

Blank Space (Taylor Swift) • Heartbeat Song (Kelly Clarkson) • I Really Like You (Carly Rae Jepsen) • I'm Not the Only One (Sam Smith) • Thinking Out Loud (Ed Sheeran).

00146286 Easy Piano $9.99

CALL ME MAYBE, HOME & MORE HOT SINGLES

Call Me Maybe (Carly Rae Jepsen) • Heart Attack (Demi Lovato) • Home (Phillip Phillips) • Just Give Me a Reason (Pink) • Next to Me (Emeli Sandé).

00121544 Easy Piano $9.99

GET LUCKY, BLURRED LINES & MORE HOT SINGLES

Blurred Lines (Robin Thicke feat. T.I. + Pharrell) • Brave (Sara Bareilles) • Cruise (Florida Georgia Line) • Cups (When I'm Gone) (Anna Kendrick) • Get Lucky (Daft Punk feat. Pharrell Williams).

00122334 Easy Piano $9.99

HELLO, BETTER WHEN I'M DANCIN' & MORE HOT SINGLES

Better When I'm Dancin' (Meghan Trainor) • Burning House (Cam) • Drag Me Down (One Direction) • Hello (Adele) • She Used to Be Mine (Sara Bareilles).

00156235 Easy Piano $9.99

HO HEY, SOME NIGHTS & MORE HOT SINGLES

Ho Hey (The Lumineers) • It's Time (Imagine Dragons) • Some Nights (fun.) • Stay (Rihanna) • When I Was Your Man (Bruno Mars).

00119861 Easy Piano $9.99

LET IT GO, HAPPY & MORE HOT SINGLES

All of Me (John Legend) • Dark Horse (Katy Perry) • Happy (Pharrell) • Let It Go (Demi Lovato) • Pompeii (Bastille).

00128204 Easy Piano $9.99

ROAR, ROYALS & MORE HOT SINGLES

Atlas (Coldplay – from *The Hunger Games: Catching Fire*) • Roar (Katy Perry) • Royals (Lorde) • Safe and Sound (Capital Cities) • Wake Me Up! (Avicii).

00123868 Easy Piano $9.99

SAY SOMETHING, COUNTING STARS & MORE HOT SINGLES

Counting Stars (One Republic) • Demons (Imagine Dragons) • Let Her Go (Passenger) • Say Something (A Great Big World) • Story of My Life (One Direction).

00125356 Easy Piano $9.99

SEE YOU AGAIN, FLASHLIGHT & MORE HOT SINGLES

Budapest (George Ezra) • Flashlight (Jessie J.) • Honey I'm Good (Andy Grammer) • See You Again (Wiz Khalifa) • Shut Up and Dance (Walk the Moon).

00150045 Easy Piano $9.99

SHAKE IT OFF, ALL ABOUT THAT BASS & MORE HOT SINGLES

All About That Bass (Meghan Trainor) • Shake It Off (Taylor Swift) • A Sky Full of Stars (Coldplay) • Something in the Water (Carrie Underwood) • Take Me to Church (Hozier).

00142734 Easy Piano $9.99

STAY WITH ME, SING & MORE HOT SINGLES

Am I Wrong? (Nico & Vinz) • Boom Clap (from *The Fault in Our Stars*) (Charli XCX) • Love Runs Out (One Republic) • Sing (Ed Sheeran) • Stay with Me (Sam Smith).

00138067 Easy Piano $9.99

Prices, contents and availability subject to change without notice.

HAL•LEONARD® CORPORATION
7777 W. BLUEMOUND RD. P.O. BOX 13819 MILWAUKEE, WI 53213
www.halleonard.com

0116